Mary and Joseph were going to have a baby. Mary had been busy making baby clothes. Joseph was a carpenter, so he made a beautiful wooden cradle. They were very happy and excited that their baby would soon be born.

tools

1

Then a message came. It said that all the people had to go to the town where they were born, to be counted and pay a tax. That meant that Mary and Joseph would have to travel far from their home to Bethlehem.

 **journey**

With such a long trip to make, they had to leave
behind the beautiful cradle and many of the soft
baby clothes. They walked and walked for many
days.

donkey

When they arrived in Bethlehem they were very tired. Joseph went to the inn to ask for a room where they could sleep. All the rooms were full. Joseph was very sad. What would they do? One of the men saw how sad Joseph looked and how tired Mary was. He said they could sleep in his barn.

4

inn door

Mary and Joseph were very thankful. They didn't mind sharing the barn with all the animals. They soon found a corner and spread out their blankets. They lay on the straw and pulled the blankets over them. It was quiet. Mary and Joseph were warm and dry. That night Mary's baby was born.

COW

5

Mary and Joseph were happy that their baby had come. The cradle Joseph made was not there. But Joseph found a manger filled with hay for the animals. "This will make a good bed for our baby Jesus," he said. Mary lovingly wrapped baby Jesus in strips of special cloth and laid him down to sleep.

manger

Not far away, out on a hillside, there were some shepherds looking after their sheep. Suddenly there was a bright light. Angel messengers sang a song of good news.

"In Bethlehem a special baby has been born. He is God's son. He will save the people." That's what the angels sang.

angel

7

The shepherds also journeyed into Bethlehem. They found Mary and Joseph and little baby Jesus who was lying in a manger, just as the angels said.

Then the shepherds returned home, thanking God for this wonderful night and all God's love.

8   *lamb*